Freckles Finds A Forever HOME

RENEE' SERVELLO

EXPLORA BOOKS
700 – 838 West Hastings St. Vancouver, BC V6C 0A6
www.explorabooks.com
Phone: (604) 330 6795

No part of this book may be reproduced, stored in a retrieval system, or transmitted by any means without the written permission of the author.

Because of the dynamic nature of the Internet, any web addresses or links contained in this book may have changed since publication and may no longer be valid. The views expressed in this work are solely those of the author and do not necessarily reflect the views of the publisher, and the publisher hereby disclaims any responsibility for them.

ISBN: 978-1-83430-097-9 (*Paperback*)

© 2025 Renee Servello. All rights reserved.

Other books by Renee' Servello

* * *

Humor All The Way
You're Kidding...I'm A Senior?

This book is dedicated to our
wonderful little peeps:
Lauren, Alexandra, Gabrielle, Lane, Preston,
Rocco and Karson.
Thank you for all of the fun!
Special thanks to our daughter Kelli for
bringing little Freckles into
our lives!

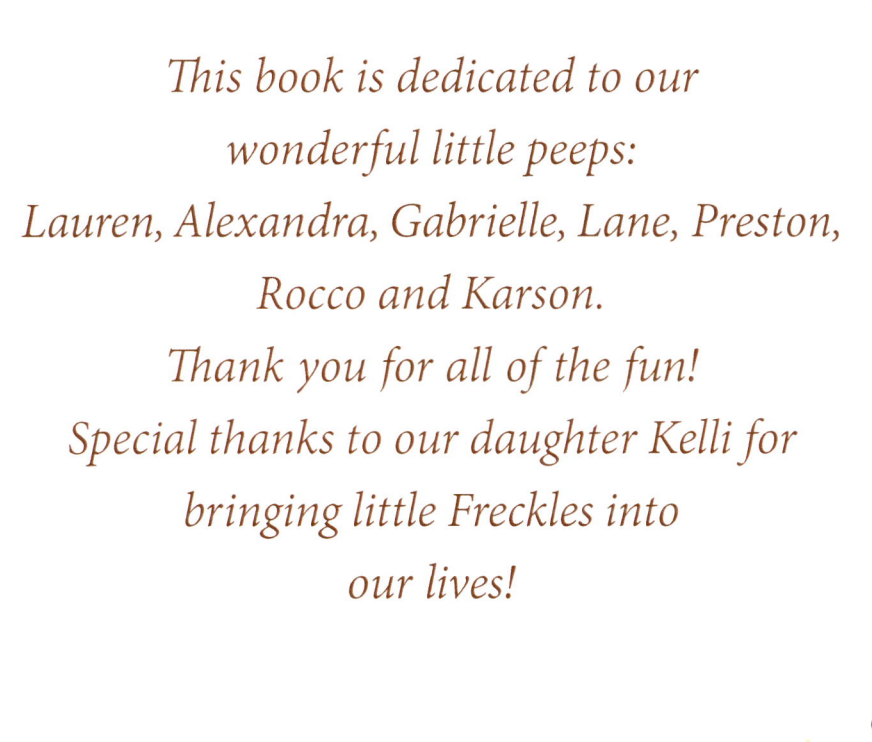

Freckles Finds A Forever HOME

I was born on a Bunny Farm in Houston, Texas. There were hundreds and hundreds of bunnies just like me.

We were stuffed in cages with each other, I really
didn't like being squeezed like that.
We all had to fight to get a drink of water or food
out of the little bottles and bowls.
Bunnies squeezed together like that are rude.
They don't take turns drinking or eating
like you are supposed to.
When I tried to take a nap, the other bunnies
would push me, step on me or hop over me.
What's a bunny to do?
I wasn't really happy at the Bunny Farm but I
thought I would always be there.

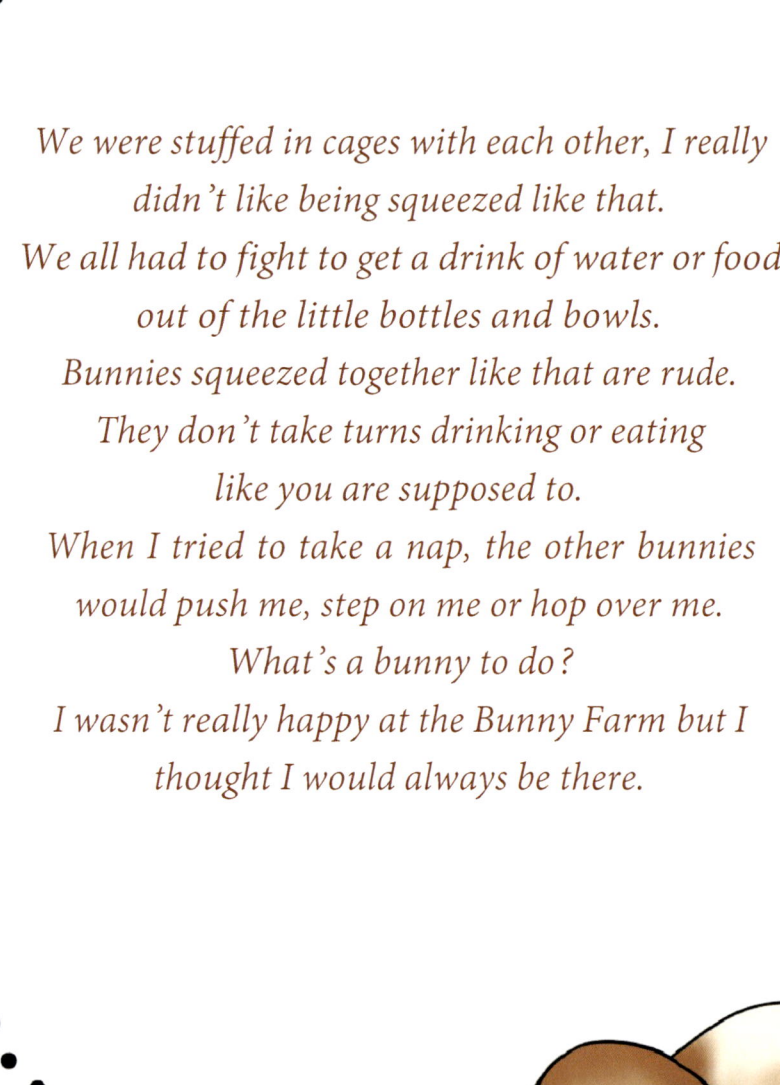

One day a strange two-legged person walked
over to my cage.
She stared at me and I thought she was very big.
She was so tall that she scared me.
I only weighed two pounds then and could fit in the
palm of her hand.
Anyway, the stranger's name was Kelli.
She was on a mission...
that means she had business to take care of.
Kelli's Mom wanted a bunny for Mother's Day. Kelli
loves her Mom so she started looking
at bunnies at the Bunny Farm.
She liked me, I think. I was the cutest bunny in the cage.
I'm white with brown spots that look like freckles.
Everyone in my cage was scared when Kelli kept looking
at us. But I knew Kelli wouldn't
hurt us, she looked pretty nice for a tall person.
I think Kelli and I just liked each other from
the first day.

*She told the Bunny Farm that she wanted
to buy me for her Mom.
The people at the Bunny Farm put me in a tiny little
cage all by myself.
That made me really scared.
Then they gave me to Kelli.*

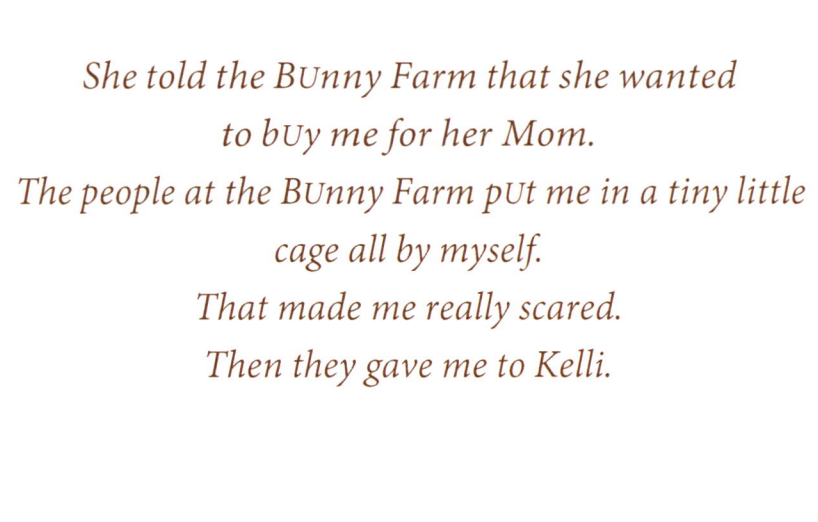

*She put my cage in her car,
I didn't know what a car was.
It made lots of noise and then it started moving. I was so scared that I wished I was back with the other bunnies.
Kelli talked and talked to me. Kelli never stops talking. After a while, I got used to hearing her talk and fell asleep. When the car stopped rolling,
I woke up...
Kelli was still talking.*

She picked my cage up and took me inside a house. She sat my cage down and a woman and a man started talking like Kelli. Everybody sure talks a lot. This was another scary day. Kelli let me with the woman and man. She said "Happy Mother's Day" to the woman.

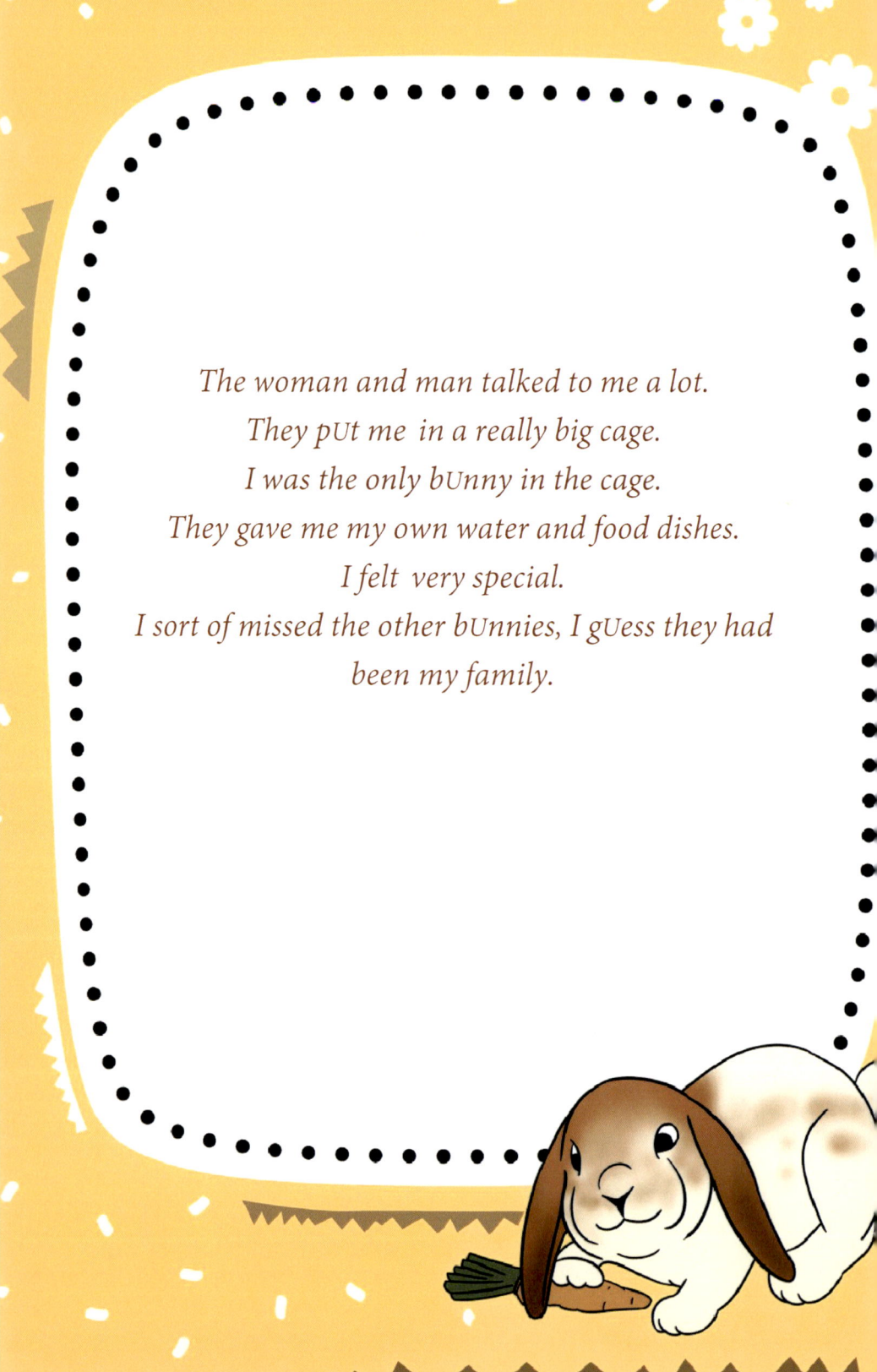

*The woman and man talked to me a lot.
They put me in a really big cage.
I was the only bunny in the cage.
They gave me my own water and food dishes.
I felt very special.
I sort of missed the other bunnies, I guess they had been my family.*

The woman and man kept talking to me and told me
that my new name was Freckles because
I looked like I had freckles all over.
They said they were my new Mom and Dad.
Actually, my Dad named me.
He's very smart.

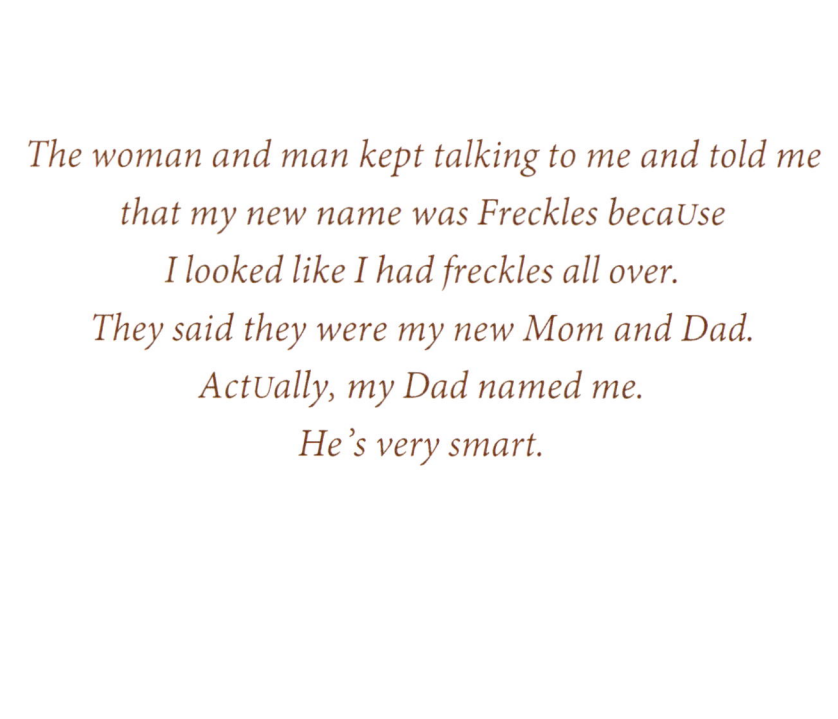

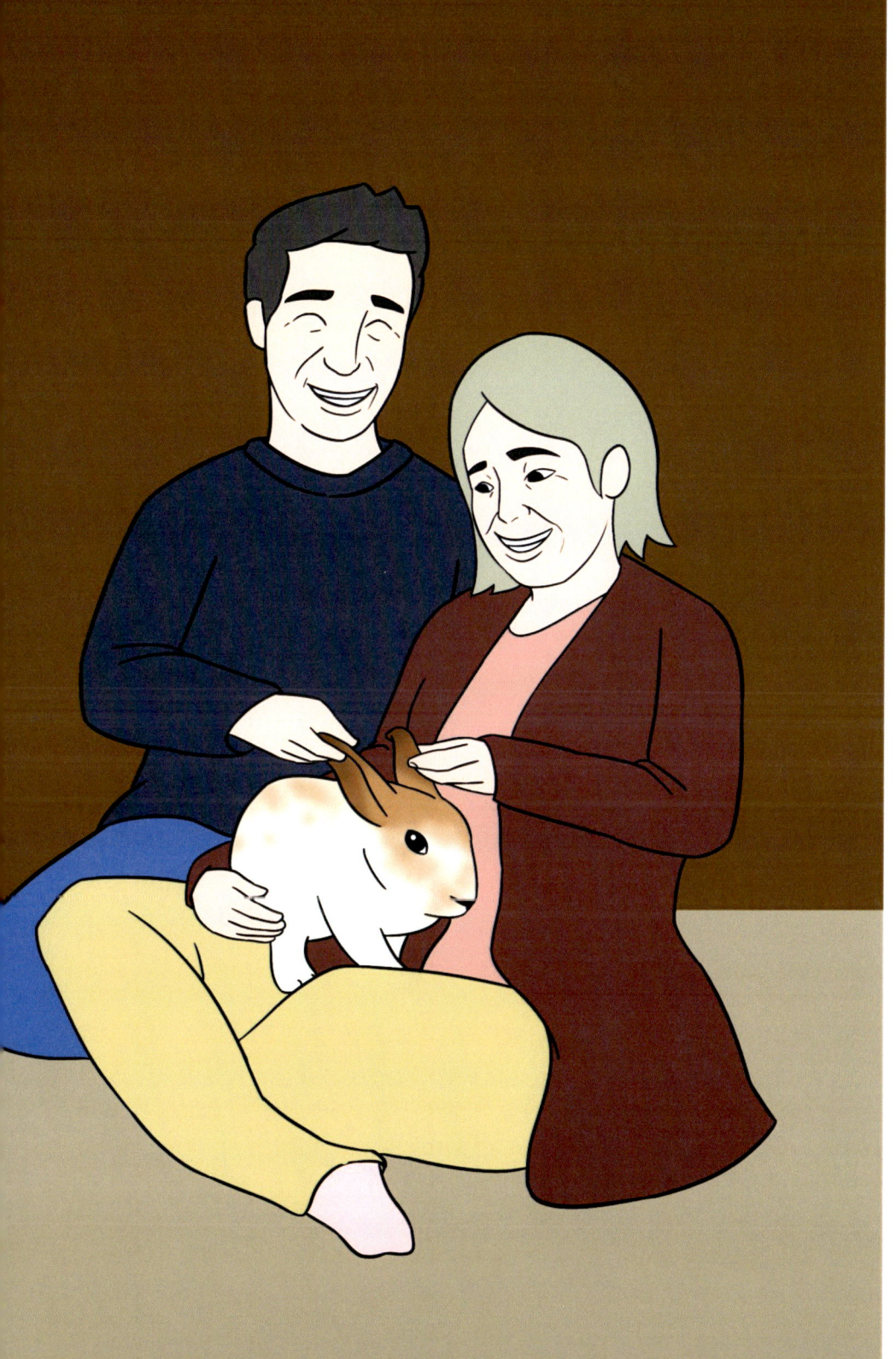

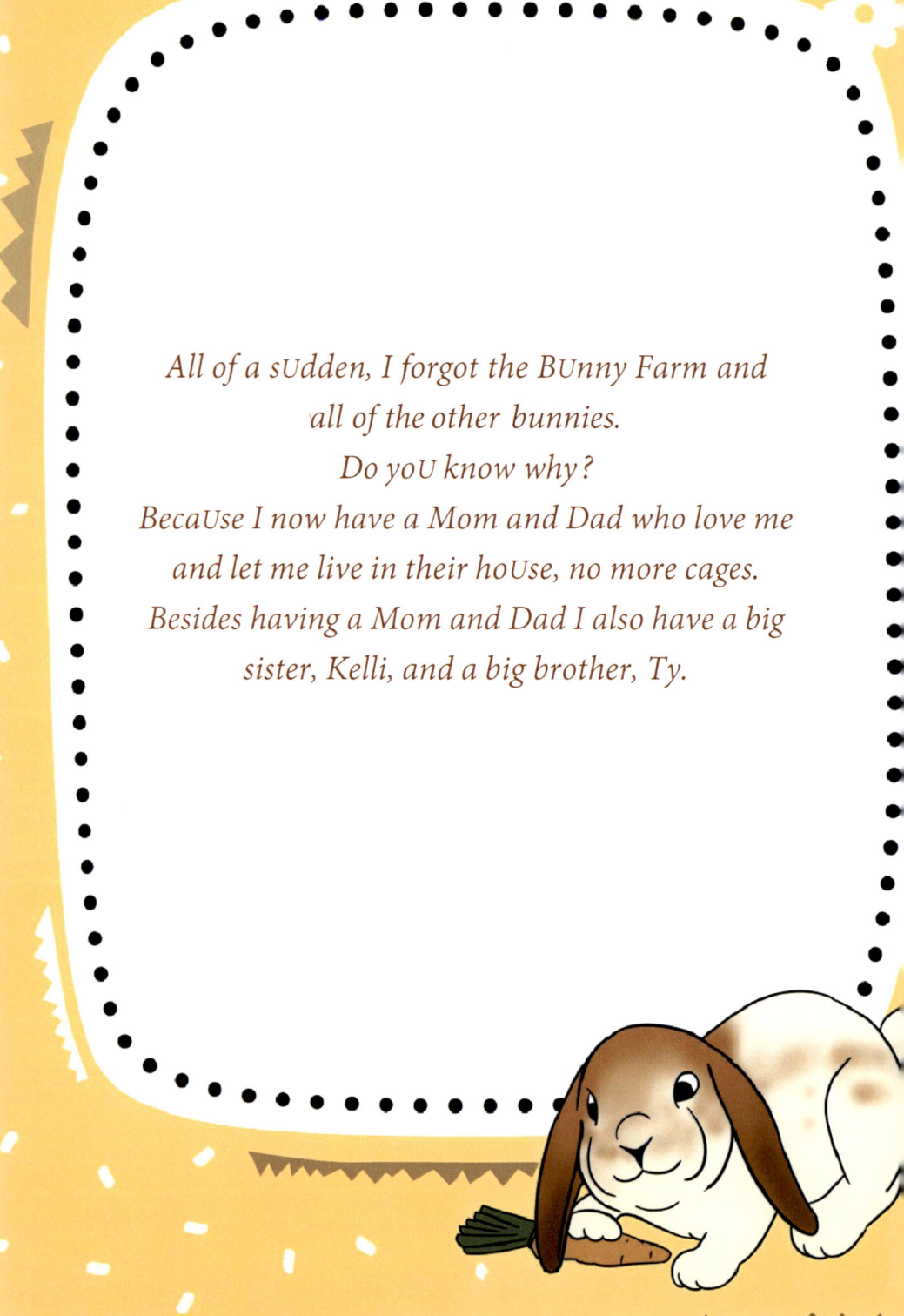

All of a sudden, I forgot the Bunny Farm and all of the other bunnies.
Do you know why?
Because I now have a Mom and Dad who love me and let me live in their house, no more cages.
Besides having a Mom and Dad I also have a big sister, Kelli, and a big brother, Ty.

*I'm so happy with my new family.
Mom and Dad are really special.
They talk to me all day and sometimes Kelli and Ty
come to visit me.
They talk, talk, talk and then
squeeze me.*

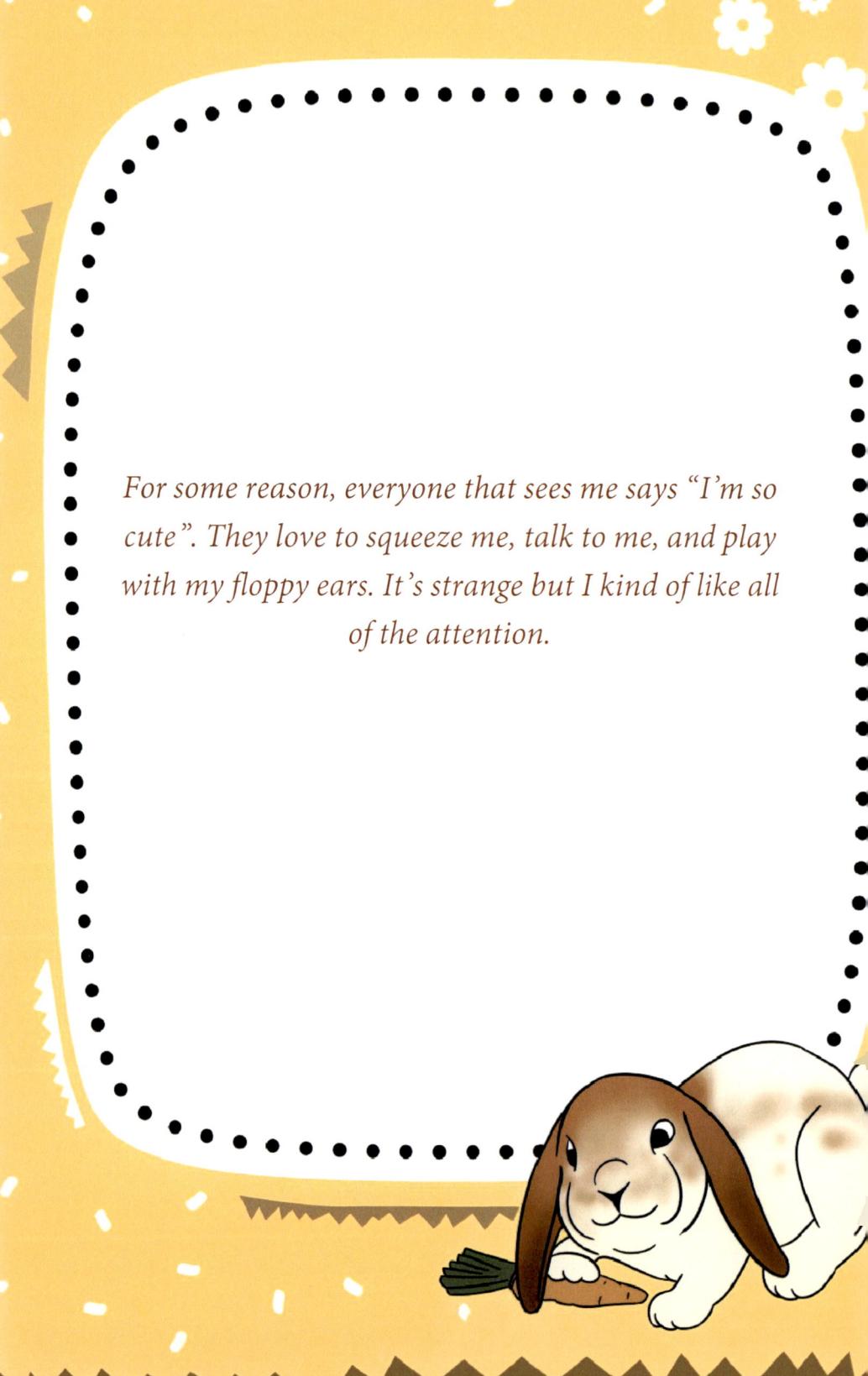

For some reason, everyone that sees me says "I'm so cute". They love to squeeze me, talk to me, and play with my floppy ears. It's strange but I kind of like all of the attention.

I'm a very lucky bunny because I now
have a special Mom
and Dad who love me very much.
Some days they get a little carried away with all
the talking, hugging, and squeezing.
I try to be patient because I know
it makes them happy.
When you live in a family you learn about being
patient, sharing, meal times, and racing to the
door when somebody rings the bell...
that means taller people are coming.
When the bell rings, that is my favorite time.
I run to our front door, stand up on my back legs
so I can see who is coming. It's mostly tall people,
not a lot of short people.

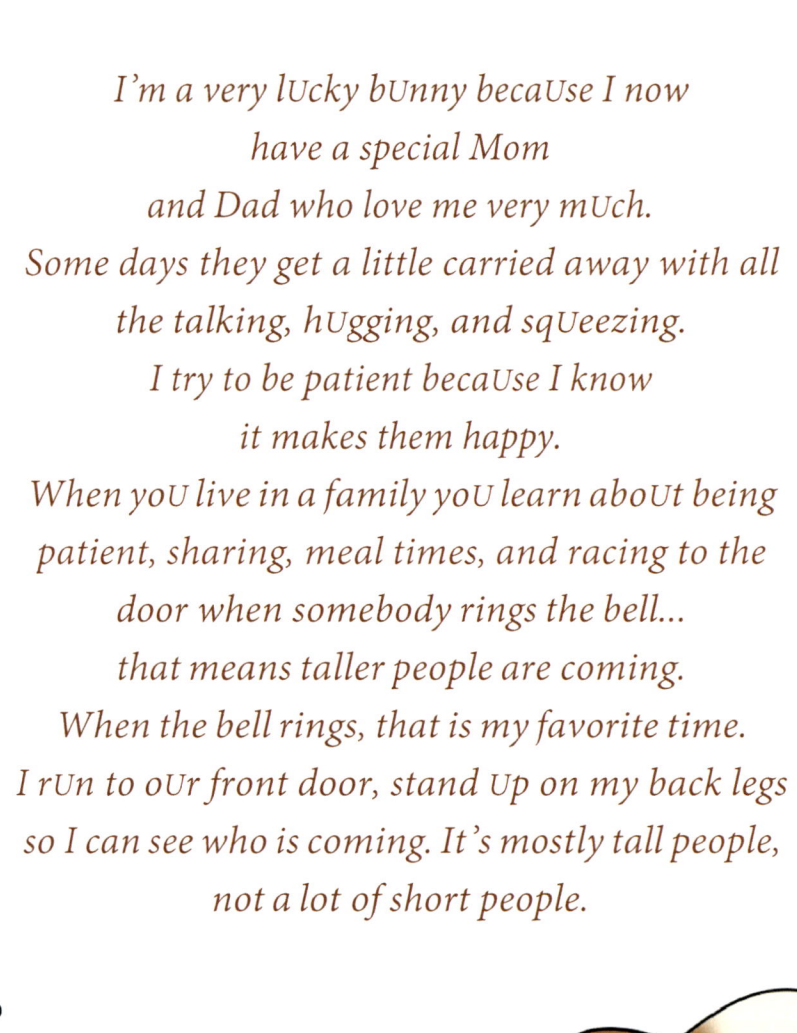

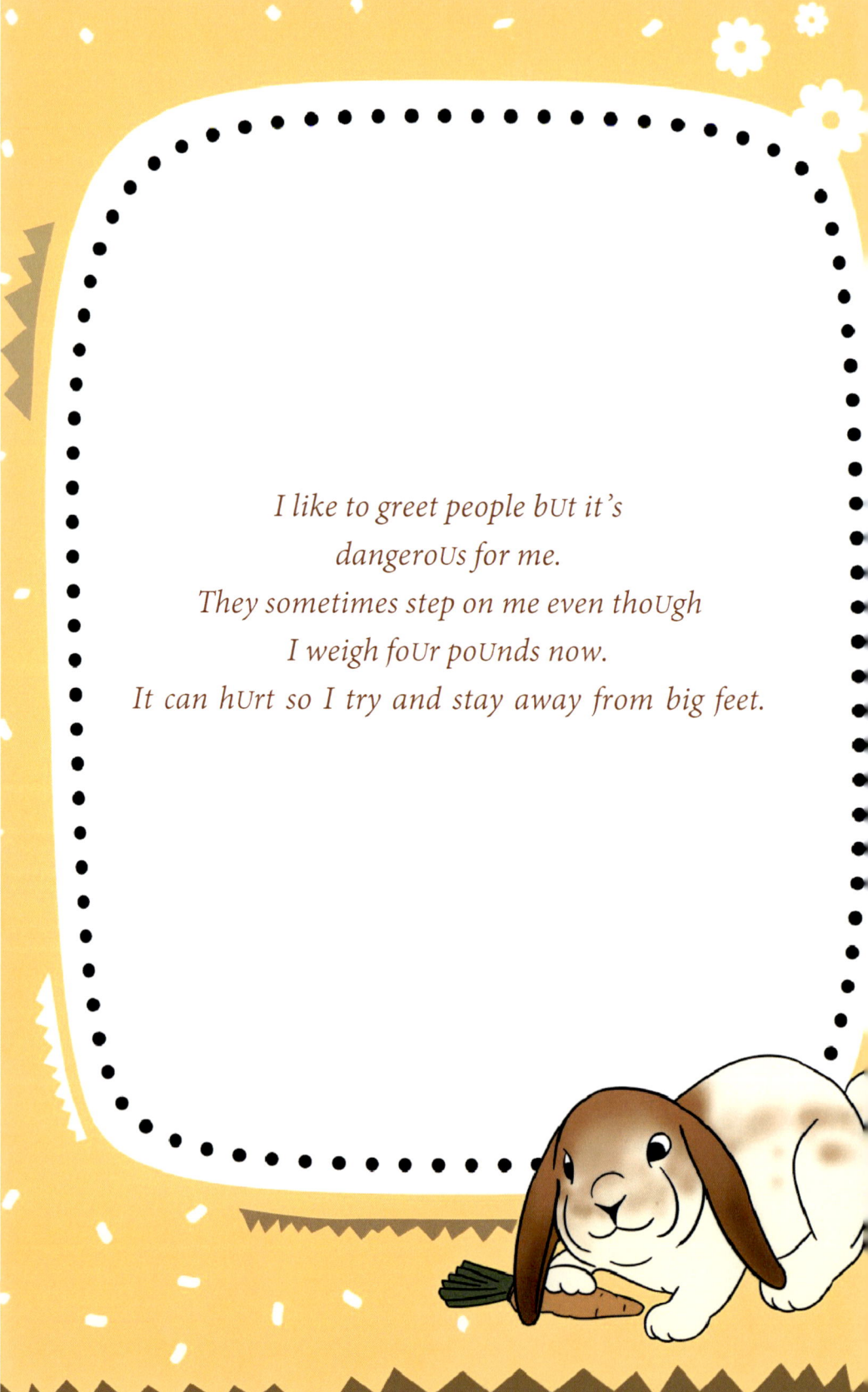

*I like to greet people bUt it's
dangeroUs for me.
They sometimes step on me even thoUgh
I weigh foUr poUnds now.
It can hUrt so I try and stay away from big feet.*

*All in all, I think my bunny life will be wonderful.
I wish my bunny friends could see me now.
Maybe they can come to visit me one day!!!!!
I may be the number one bunny but bunnies
have to learn the rules.
Sometimes it's hard to remember everything but I try.
My Mom and Dad gave me a big cage and
leave the door open.
That's pretty neat, I can hop in and out of the
cage all day long.
They put my water and food dishes in my cage.
When I have to go potty, I'm supposed to hop in my cage and
use the cage, that's a rule.
My house is two stories tall. Wow!
That means a lot of hopping.
One day, I hopped up the stairs,
I wanted to go exploring.
My Mom and Dad didn't know I could hop upstairs.
Boy, when I got upstairs, I didn't know which way to hop.
I decided to just hop and hop and see every room.
It was pretty fun but it sure wore me out.*

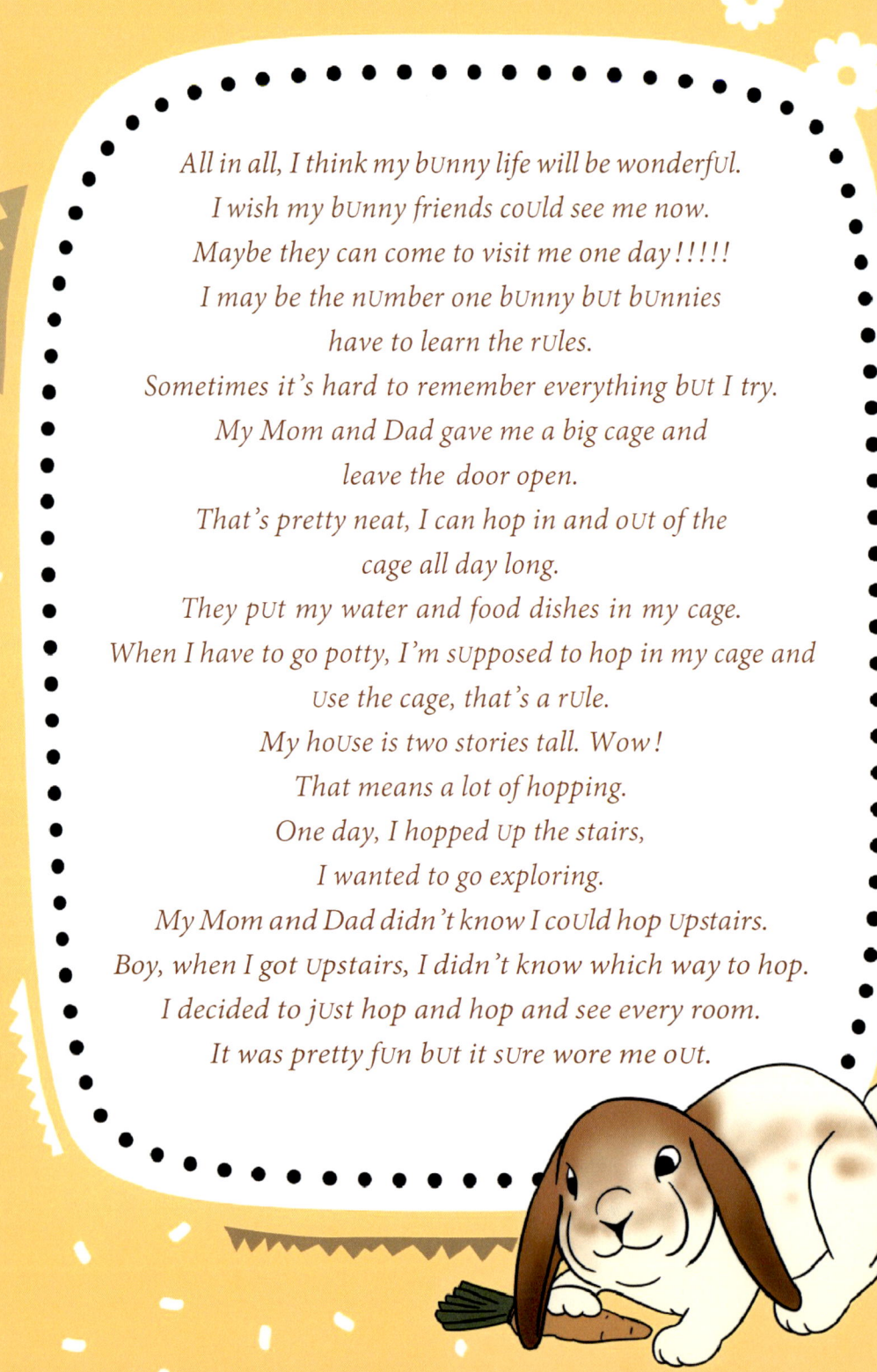

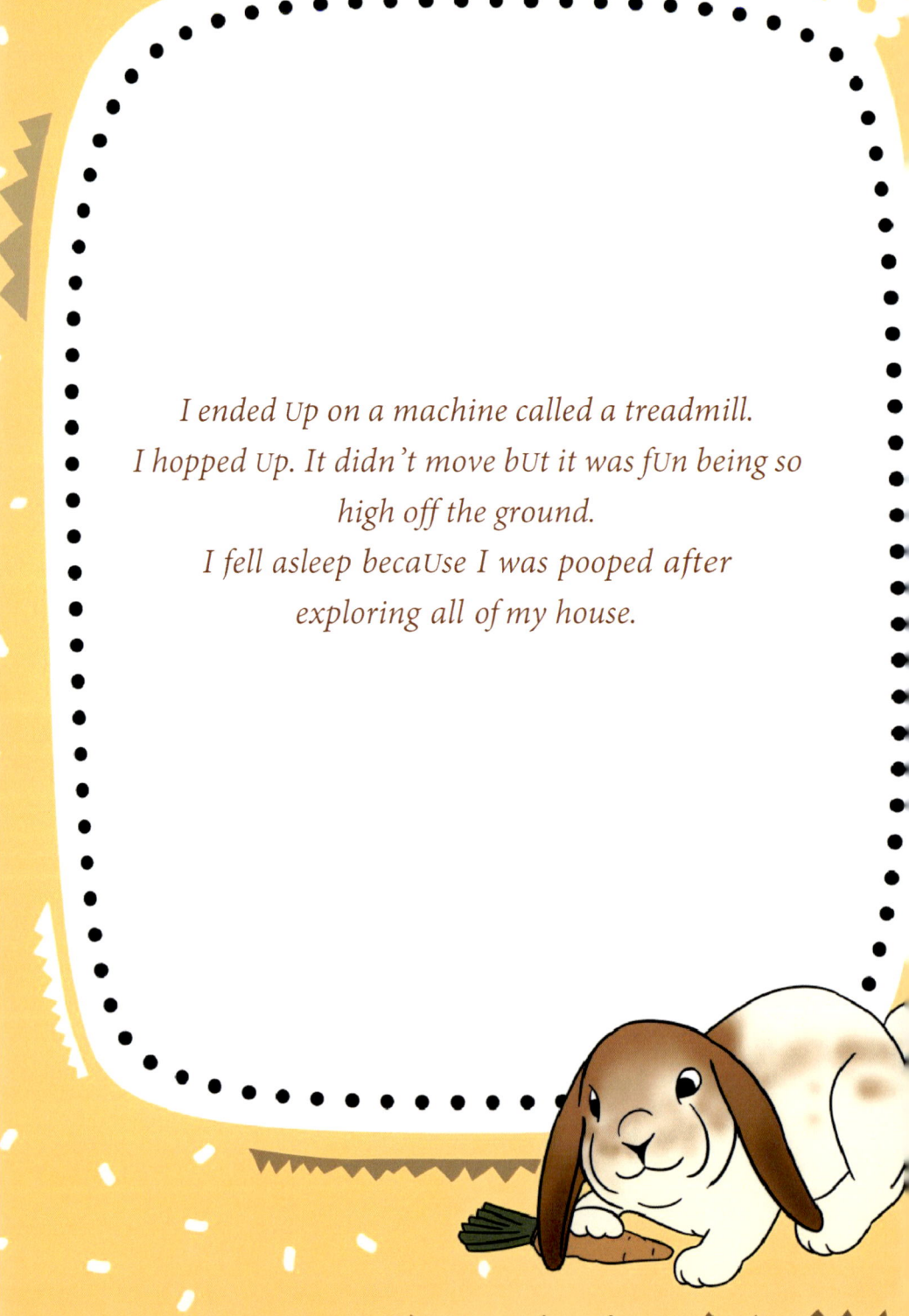

I ended up on a machine called a treadmill.
I hopped up. It didn't move but it was fun being so high off the ground.
I fell asleep because I was pooped after exploring all of my house.

All of a sudden, I heard Mom hollering to my Dad.
They thought I was lost because they
couldn't find me.
I just stayed where I was, on the treadmill waiting
for them to find me.
It took a very long time.
Finally, they came into the room where the treadmill
was and saw me sitting on it.
They picked me up and squeezed me very hard.
That means they love me.
I'm used to being squeezed.
Then they told me I couldn't go upstairs so down the
stairs I went.

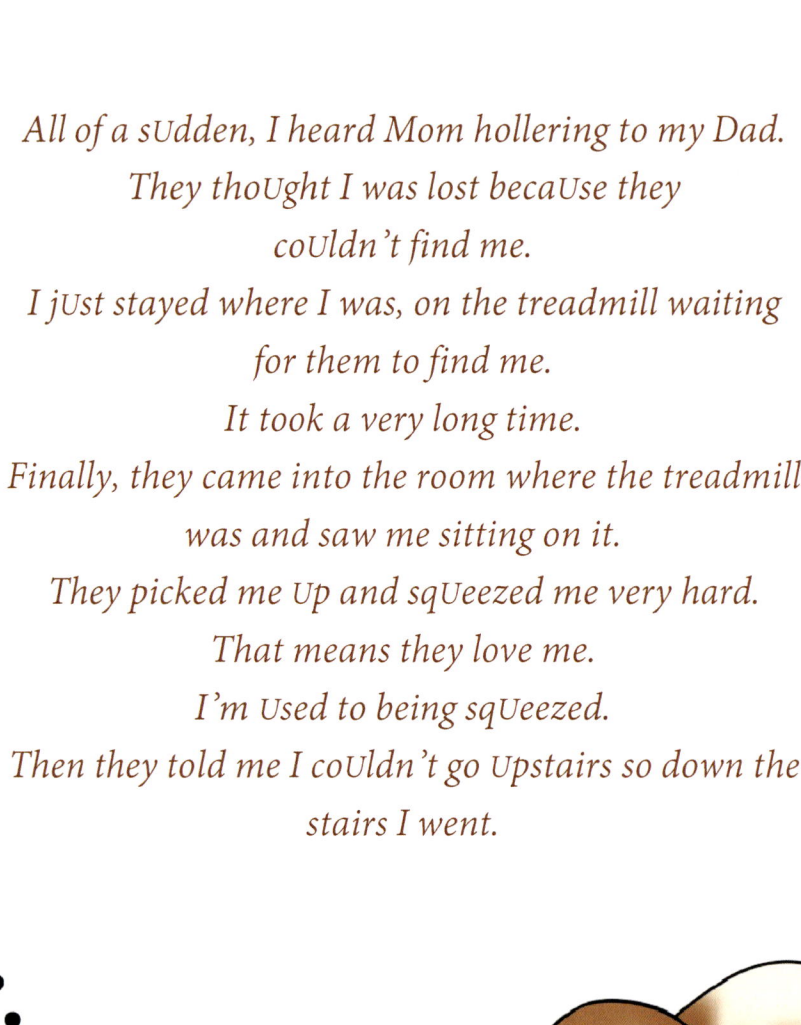

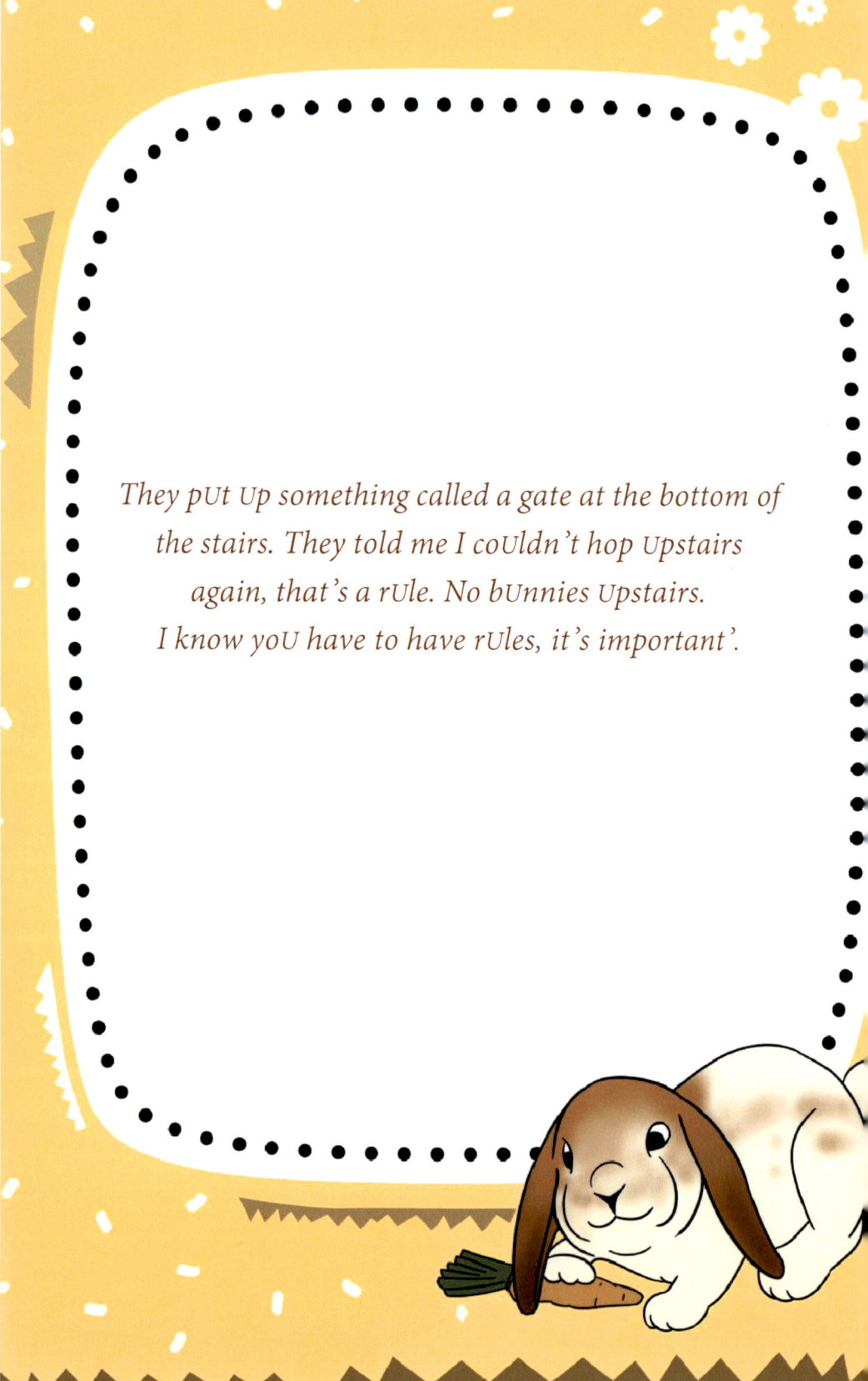

They put up something called a gate at the bottom of the stairs. They told me I couldn't hop upstairs again, that's a rule. No bunnies upstairs. I know you have to have rules, it's important'.

I weighed two poUnds when I came to live with Mom and Dad. I weigh foUr poUnds now.
I'll never get any bigger becaUse I'm a miniatUre DUtch Lop bUnny. MiniatUre means very small.
It's pretty fUnny when I hop becaUse I have floppy ears. That means that when I hop my ears flop.
Everyone say's I'm adorable...that means cUte. The more adorable yoU are the more people want to sqUeeze yoU. That means love.
Boy, do I get a lot of love.

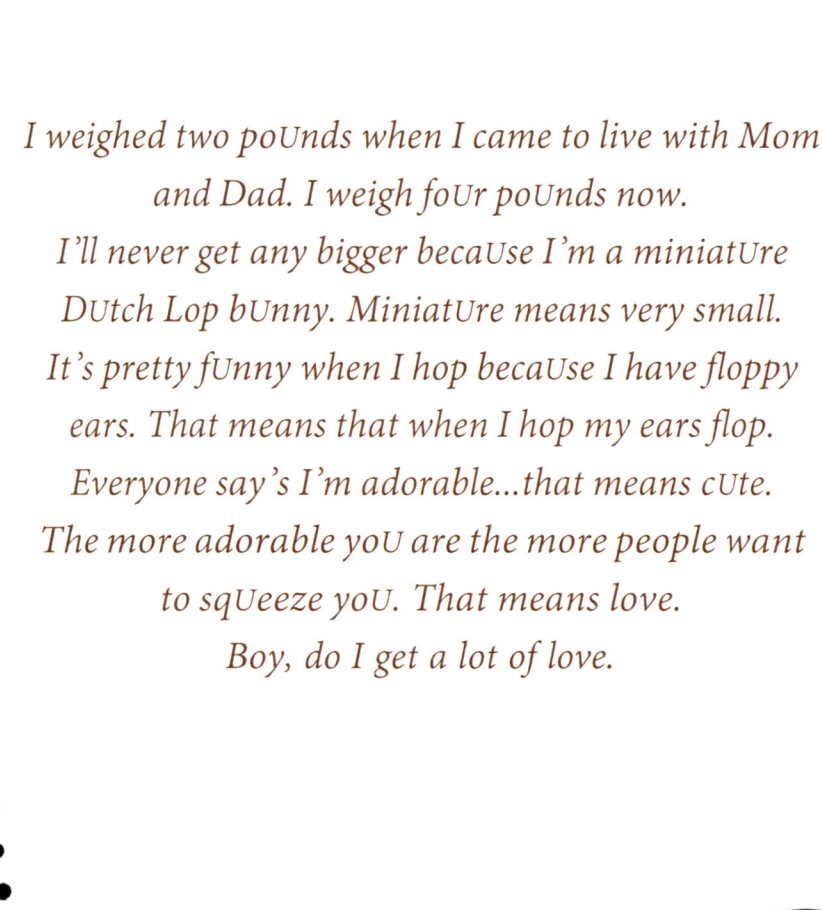

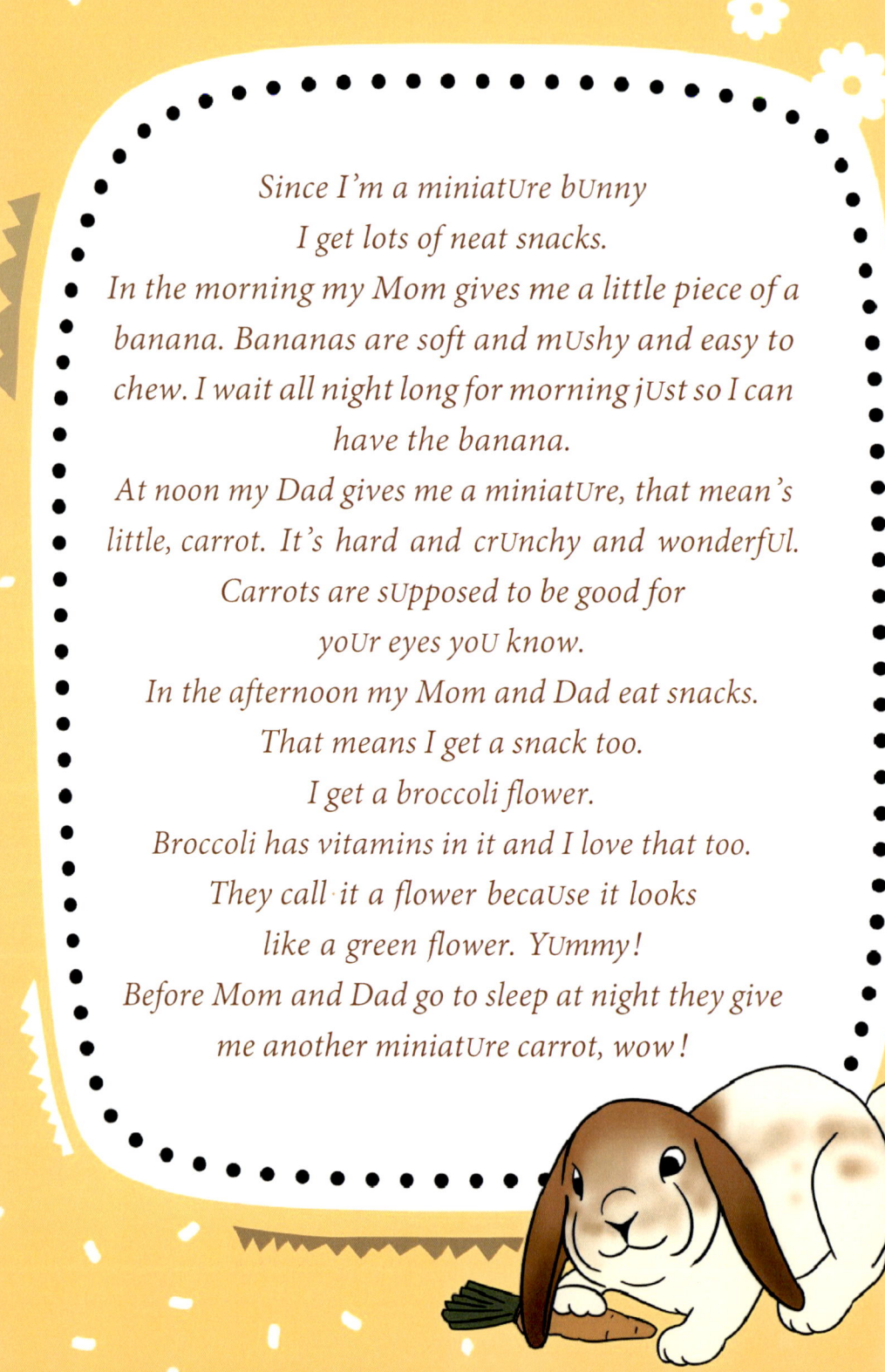

Since I'm a miniature bunny
I get lots of neat snacks.
In the morning my Mom gives me a little piece of a banana. Bananas are soft and mushy and easy to chew. I wait all night long for morning just so I can have the banana.
At noon my Dad gives me a miniature, that mean's little, carrot. It's hard and crunchy and wonderful. Carrots are supposed to be good for
your eyes you know.
In the afternoon my Mom and Dad eat snacks.
That means I get a snack too.
I get a broccoli flower.
Broccoli has vitamins in it and I love that too.
They call it a flower because it looks
like a green flower. Yummy!
Before Mom and Dad go to sleep at night they give me another miniature carrot, wow!

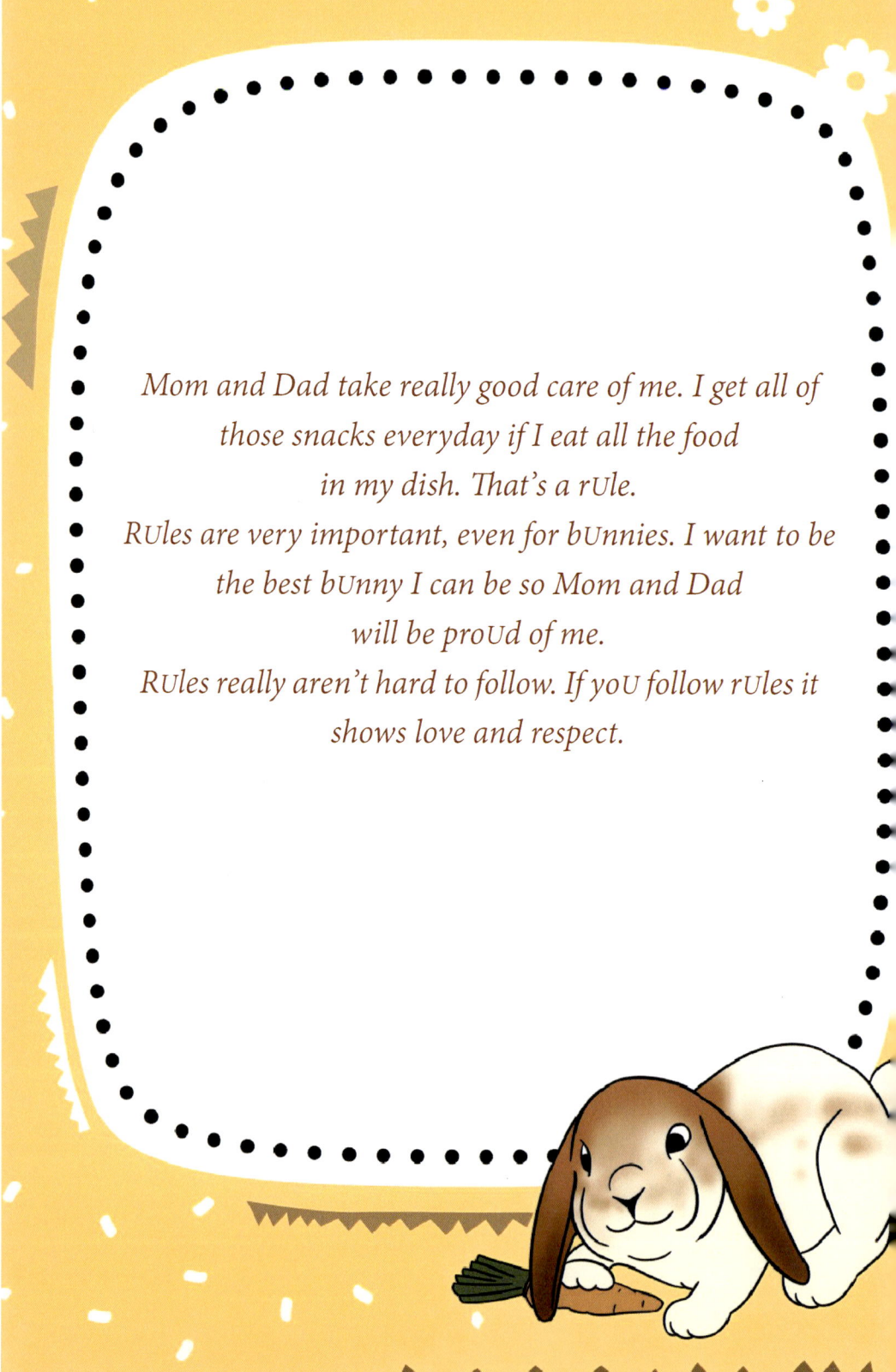

Mom and Dad take really good care of me. I get all of those snacks everyday if I eat all the food in my dish. That's a rUle.

RUles are very important, even for bUnnies. I want to be the best bUnny I can be so Mom and Dad will be proUd of me.

RUles really aren't hard to follow. If yoU follow rUles it shows love and respect.

www.ingramcontent.com/pod-product-compliance
Lightning Source LLC
Chambersburg PA
CBRC091204070526
44584CB00007B/332